Thank you to Mr. Gerald Vairo, head of the restoration project for the
George Gipp Memorial in Laurium, Michigan, for his expertise and
knowledge regarding the life of George Gipp, and as well, a great note of
thanks to Mr. Joel Myler, ND '88, for supplying me with supporting
documentation and help along the way. In addition, thanks to my husband
Ed, for helping me understand the finer points of football, to editors
Heather Hughes and Barb McNally for their commitment to excellence
with every book, and as always, to my son Jake for listening, reading,
and providing input every step of the way.

—*Kathy-jo*

Text Copyright © 2004 Kathy-jo Wargin
Illustration Copyright © 2004 Bruce Langton

Sleeping Bear Press
310 North Main Street, Suite 300
Chelsea, MI 48118
www.sleepingbearpress.com

THOMSON
★
GALE ™

© 2004 Thomson Gale, a part of the Thomson Corporation.

Thomson, Star Logo and Sleeping Bear Press are trademarks
and Gale is a registered trademark used herein under license.

Printed and bound in Canada.

10 9 8 7 6 5 4 3 2 1

Library of Congress Cataloging-in-Publication Data

Wargin, Kathy-jo.
Win one for the Gipper : America's football hero / written by Kathy-jo Wargin ;
illustrated by Bruce Langton.
p. cm.
ISBN 1-58536-221-2
1. Gipp, George, 1895-1920. 2. Football players—United States—Biography.
3. University of Notre Dame—Football. I. Title.
GV939.G53W37 2004
796.332'092—dc22   2004005953

My heartfelt dedication goes to my dear friend Matt Anderson.
He was the model for all the illustrations of George Gipp in this book and was also
my total inspiration and motivation in making this project a complete success.
Matt Anderson, 18 years young, died from an auto accident on April 2, 2004.
He will go on living through his family, friends, and this book.
I love you, Matt...You will stay in my heart forever.
Thanks for being a part of our life.

Bruce & family

★

Like most boys who lived in northern Michigan during the early 1900s, George Gipp played basketball and baseball and football.

From the time he was a small boy, George ran faster than most everyone. He could throw a ball farther too, and because he could dash and dodge on a dime, no one could ever catch him.

When George was older, baseball was his game. People came from miles around to watch him crack the ball over the fence and run the bases in one easy move.

George was such a talented baseball player that when he became a young man he was awarded a scholarship to the University of Notre Dame. This meant a free education as long as he played baseball for the school. So in the autumn of 1916, George left home for South Bend, Indiana. When he stepped onto campus for the first time, George didn't know what to expect.

One day after class, George and a schoolmate were kicking a football around for fun. It did not take Knute Rockne, the assistant football coach, much time to notice George. George kicked the ball high and straight, and then tossed it far and steady, never missing his target.

From not too far away Knute, or "Rock" as people called him, stood admiring the young man. He seemed to be all bone and muscle, yet quick and light on his feet.

"What's your name?" asked Rock.

"Gipp. George Gipp."

Then Rock asked George if he played football in high school and George replied,

"No, don't particularly care for football. Baseball's my dish."

"Well," invited Rock, "put on a football suit tomorrow and come out with the freshman scrubs. I think I'll make you a football player."

Deciding to give it a chance, George showed up for practice the next day. Once on the field, he raced like a runaway colt, dodging his way through players to make a touchdown. As everyone watched in amazement, George decided he liked playing football and joined the team.

In one of the early season games Notre Dame was matched against Western State Normal. Notre Dame and Western were tied at 7–7. With less than three minutes left, the Notre Dame quarterback was happy to settle for a tie score so he told George to punt, which means to kick the ball only a short distance.

But George didn't want to settle for a tie, so he asked the quarterback if he could drop-kick the ball for a win. Although the quarterback urged him to punt, George lined up the ball and thought about winning. He pulled his foot back and drop-kicked the pigskin with all his might. The ball sailed for 62 yards, soaring over the crossbar for 3 points and giving Notre Dame the win of 10 to 7! At that moment Knute Rockne knew George had a special gift. George Gipp played not only with his body and mind; he also played with his heart.

The next day George's dropkick made headlines across the nation as one of the longest in recorded history. Everyone thought George Gipp was a football sensation!

And George became a sensation off the field, too. When he wasn't playing football or going to class, he played pool or card games with people from town. Sometimes, if he won money, he bought dinner for people who didn't have enough to eat.

The students of Notre Dame, the people of South Bend, and football fans across the nation loved George Gipp. And George Gipp loved football. Although it was baseball that brought George to college, he decided that football was the sport he would play at Notre Dame.

In 1918, George's second season, Knute Rockne became head coach of the team. He and George grew to be good friends and football partners. Game after game, George was unstoppable on the field.

In October of 1920, George's fourth and final year at Notre Dame, the team traveled to the United States Military Academy at West Point. Tension filled the air as the Notre Dame players prepared to meet their longstanding rival, the Army team.

As both teams entered the field, the stadium filled with cheers. But when the game began, the Notre Dame players were met with one crushing blow after another. At halftime the tired Notre Dame team was down 14-17, and it looked like they were going to lose.

But George wasn't going to let that happen. When he came out in the second half he came out fighting like a giant. With quick passes and pounding tackles, George delivered at every step, advancing his team forward. In the final quarter Notre Dame made a touchdown and George kicked for an extra point, setting the score at 21 to 17. But George wanted more. With a fake criss-cross play, Gipp and his teammates made one more touchdown.

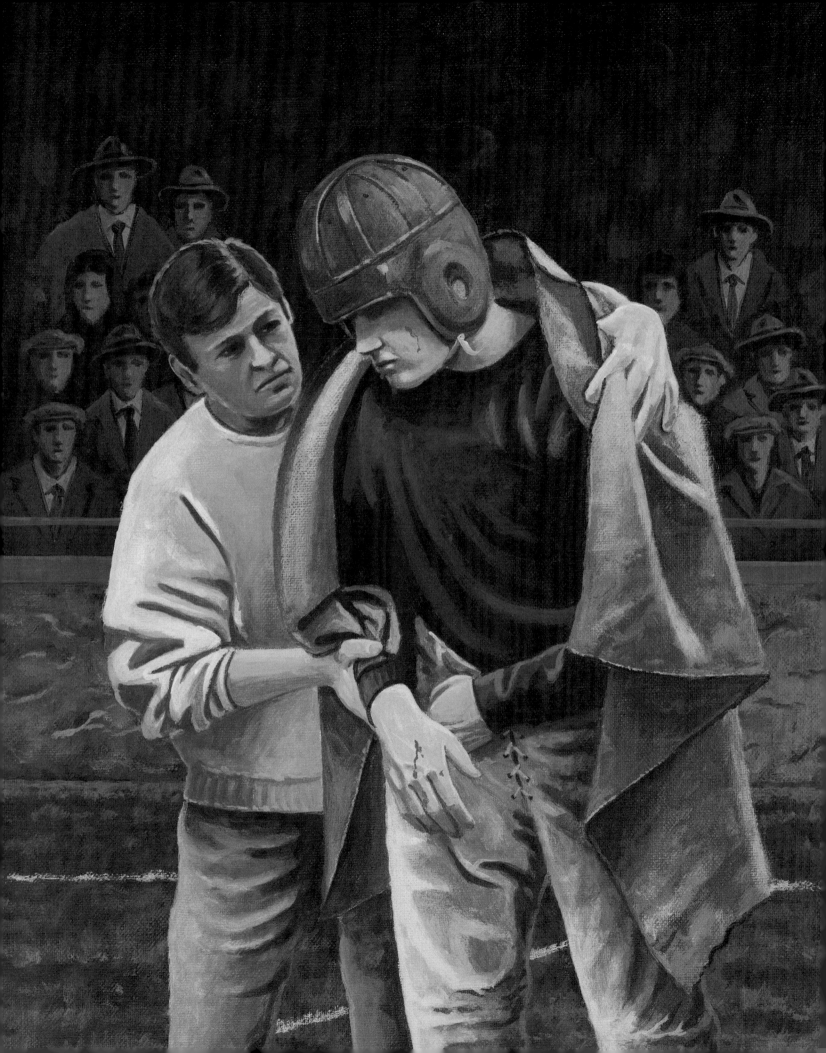

With moments left and a win apparent, Knute called George out of the game so he could rest. George staggered toward the sidelines, tired, bloody, and satisfied. And as he stepped off the field, the entire crowd in the stadium came to their feet without making a sound. Nobody applauded and nobody cheered. Both sides were in such awe of the mighty George Gipp that they honored him with a silent tribute.

The next day, newspaper headlines around the country said George Gipp was one of the best football players ever.

But several games later, as the team prepared for a game against Northwestern University, George was not feeling well. His throat was sore, his body weak, and he had a fever. Knute was worried. He told George that if he wasn't feeling better when they got to the game, he would not be expected to play.

When they arrived for the game, George still was not feeling well, so he sat on the sidelines. But the day had been reserved as "George Gipp Day," and people had come from all over to see him play. Wrapped in a wool blanket, George shook from chills and burning fever. But since they didn't know he was sick, fans began to grumble when they saw him on the sidelines.

During the game, a few voices started to call "We want Gipp! We want Gipp!" It wasn't long before more voices joined in and soon the whole crowd was calling for George to play.

The wind was ice-cutting cold and George's throat felt sharp and burning tight. But he did not want to disappoint the crowd. Near the end of the game, George removed the blanket and slowly stepped onto the field to the sound of great cheers. Joining the other players, and gathering all the strength he could muster, he worked to make a perfect pass for 35 yards and a touchdown. Minutes later he threw another pass, this time good for 70 yards.

But inside, George was growing weaker by the minute.

Two days later, a very sick George showed up at a banquet being held to honor the Notre Dame football team. The pain and fever had worsened, so he told Knute that he needed to get to the hospital. By the time they arrived, George was a very sick young man.

The doctors said George had a bad case of tonsillitis. One week later the hospital bulletin stated he had pneumonia and a serious throat infection. Across the nation, newspapers sent out word of George's condition, and reporters camped outside the hospital for updates.

Meanwhile, George had been named to the All-American team, one of the greatest football honors ever. But George was too sick to celebrate the good news.

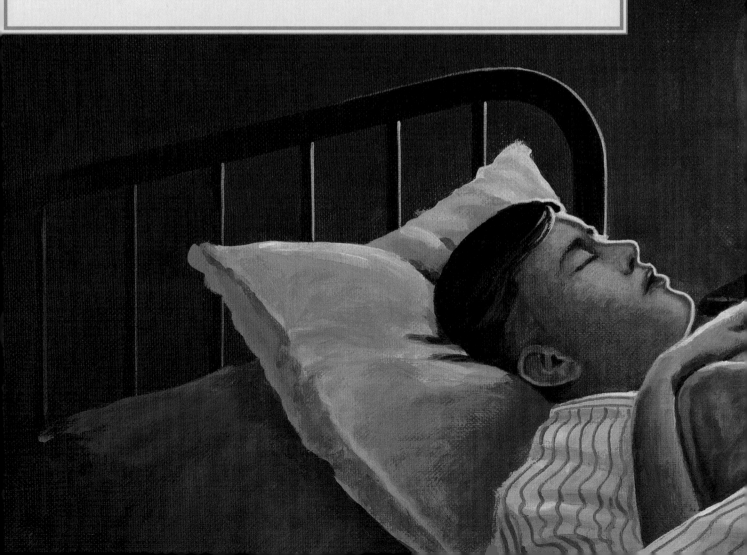

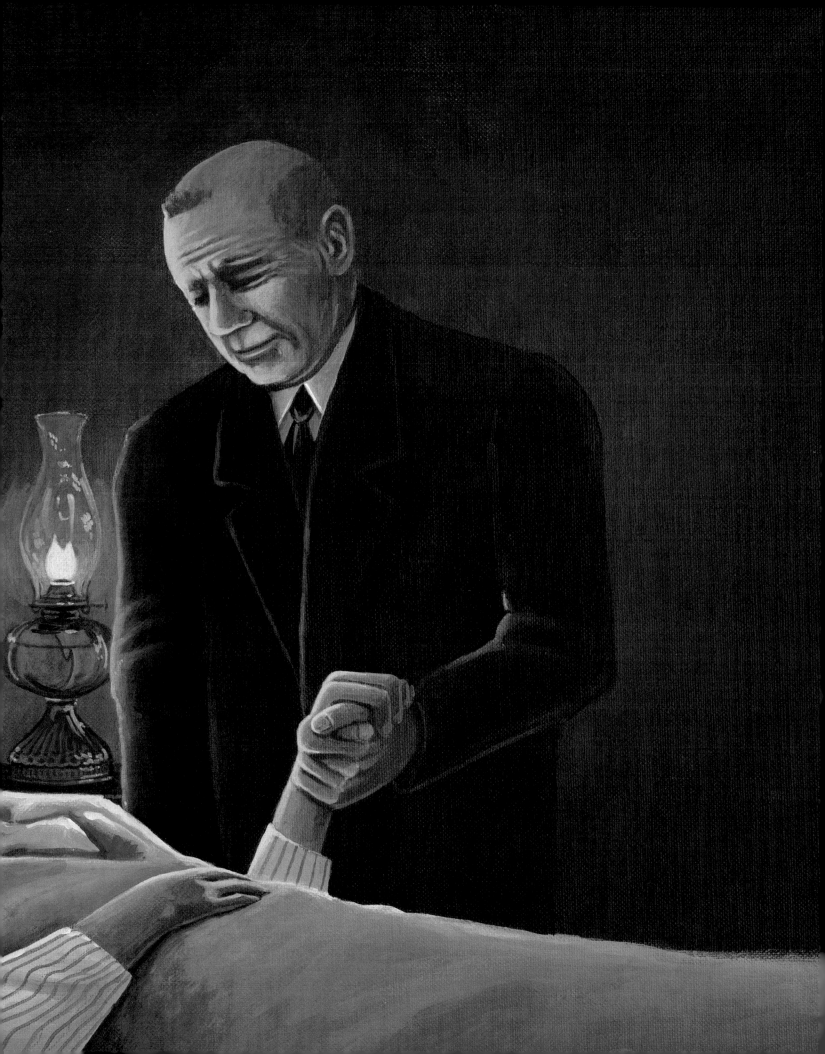

In his Michigan hometown, the local newspaper office printed cards with news about George and displayed them in the window, changing them throughout the day. As people walked by, they could read about his progress.

While George remained in the hospital, Knute was a regular visitor. Over the next two weeks, he watched as George's condition grew worse and the once strong, muscular young man became thin and pale.

One night, as his family and Knute stood quietly by, George motioned for Knute to come closer. Then, as Knute leaned down to his friend, George whispered something into his ear.

Hours later, the card in the newspaper window of George's hometown simply said *George Gipp Died*.

Knute Rockne didn't tell anyone what George Gipp said before he passed away. Keeping true to George's last request, he waited for just the right moment to let George's final thoughts be known.

And eight years later that moment came.

Knute was still the head coach and his Notre Dame team was struggling against the West Point Army cadets, the rival team George always loved to beat. The Notre Dame team, lacking in spirit, drive, and strength, was behind during the first half and a win looked hopeless. So at halftime Knute called the team together in a huddle on the locker room floor. The boys were feeling beaten, tired, and discouraged as Knute began to speak.

"Boys, I want to tell you a story. I never thought I would have to tell it, but the time has come."

Then he told them what George Gipp whispered to him right before he died.

"I've got to go, Rock. It's all right. I'm not afraid. Sometime, Rock, when the team is up against it, when things are wrong and the breaks are beating the boys, tell them to go in there with all they've got and win just one for the Gipper. I don't know where I'll be then, Rock, but I'll know about it, and I'll be happy."

The players fell silent as the spirit of George Gipp filled the room. The young men thought about his last words, and fought against their own tears. And right then, Knute looked them straight on and said,

"This is the day, and you are that team."

With a roar of determination, Notre Dame exploded onto the field for the second half. The team worked its way down the field until they neared their opponents' end zone. On fourth down, Notre Dame lined up on the one-yard line and the fullback was handed the ball. He plunged hard into the end zone where he slammed himself and the ball to the ground.

And as that ball hit the grass, he yelled out the words that would become legendary,

"That's one for the Gipper!"

With new life, the inspired Notre Dame team went on to beat Army at West Point.

And that's one for the Gipper...for always.

ABOUT THE STORY

GEORGE GIPP was born in 1895, in a Michigan Upper Peninsula mining town called Laurium. His story is one where history and legend will forever be intertwined.

George Gipp went to the University of Notre Dame on a baseball scholarship (and even played on the basketball team in 1919), but at Knute Rockne's urging, tried out for football and made the team. It wasn't long before George left the baseball team and went on to become one of the finest football players to play for Notre Dame—or any football team.

When he wasn't playing football for Notre Dame, George still played baseball in leagues outside the school, and was under contract for a tryout with the Chicago Cubs baseball team when he died of pneumonia and strep throat in December 1920. At that time, people often died of such illnesses because there were no antibiotics such as penicillin.

At six feet and 175 pounds, George played halfback and could run 100 yards in 10.2 seconds. Walter Camp, the football innovator who is today known as the "father" of American football, selected him as Notre Dame's first player to the All-American Team.

George held a career mark of 2,341 rushing yards, a record that lasted more than 50 years. As a defensive back, he never allowed a completed pass in his territory. In 1951, George was voted into the College Football Hall of Fame.

Off the field, George was like many young men of his era; he enjoyed playing cards and shooting pool, and at times used money earned from those games to help friends pay for school. His story is one of inspiration, courage, and passion for life.

"The Gipper" will always remain a young man from Michigan's Upper Peninsula whose life was treasured by so many, and whose loss was mourned by an entire nation.

And forever, he will be remembered as the legend of Notre Dame, America's football hero.

—Kathy-jo Wargin